A History of the Theories of Rain

Also By Stephen Collis

Poetry
Anarchive
*The Commons**
Decomp (with Jordan Scott)
Mine
*On the Material**
*Once in Blockadia**
*To the Barricades**

Fiction
The Red Album

Non-Fiction
*Almost Islands: Phyllis Webb and the Pursuit of the Unwritten**
*Dispatches from the Occupation: A History of Change**
*Phyllis Webb and the Common Good: Poetry / Anarchy /
    Abstraction**
Through Words of Others: Susan Howe and Anarcho-Scholasticism

As Editor
*Reading Duncan Reading: Robert Duncan and the Poetics of
    Derivation* (with Graham Lyons)
Taking Measures: Selected Serial Poems, by George Bowering*

* Published by Talonbooks

A HISTORY OF THE THEORIES OF RAIN

Poems

STEPHEN COLLIS

Talonbooks

Talonbooks
9259 Shaughnessy Street, Vancouver, British Columbia, Canada v6p 6r4
talonbooks.com

Talonbooks is located on xʷməθkʷəy̓əm, Sḵwx̱wú7mesh, and səl̓ilwətaʔɬ Lands.

First printing: 2021

Typeset in Arno
Printed and bound in Canada on 100% post-consumer recycled paper

Interior and cover design by Typesmith
Cover and inside cover image: Thames Barrier by William Warby via Flickr
(cc by 2.0) https://wwarby.com

Talonbooks acknowledges the financial support of the Canada Council for the Arts, the Government of Canada through the Canada Book Fund, and the Province of British Columbia through the British Columbia Arts Council and the Book Publishing Tax Credit.

Library and Archives Canada Cataloguing in Publication

Title: A history of the theories of rain : poems / Stephen Collis.
Names: Collis, Stephen, 1965– author.
Identifiers: Canadiana 20200305735 | ISBN 9781772012880 (softcover)
Classification: LCC PS8555.04938 H57 2021 | DDC C811/.54—dc23

The disaster is here, it is just not evenly distributed.

—Teju Cole

Give me music because

I never could understand its

direct connection to

that feeling stream

squall and water clock

washing ideas right out of me

taking up the mechanisms

of consanguinity rushing

toward last light over Pacific

and some seabird there

gliding and catching moonlight

same as struck only dinosaurs

to have survived last

collapse of intricate order

winging now into night

as the cellos soar and

the possibility of song remains

without words to smother it

FUTURE
IMPERFECT

So what will happen between this unusually rainless November and an unspecified but nearing future when it will have warmed however many degrees Celsius above this present stretching global mean / asking for a friend

I feel tense give me a / tense such as actions that will be completed before some other event in the future / plot a line A (present) – B (future) / and place the *future perfect* somewhere between those points / but who knows what ontological status B has now is the problem

If we don't know where we are going how will we know when we've gone too far / #capitalism / to make our *future perfect* there must be a deadline we work toward / now to then / the breach coming between we choose I choose you I choose all of you let's do this now and then

Say / we will always have been living in the future like this / say / we will have always been pondering the course of history unfolding / say / our descendants will have always been thinking / *what were they thinking* / when thinking about us in all those thoughtful days to come / but

The future is imperfect and tense / the deadlines will pass and still some will be dreaming states of continuity / I want to state some continuity / look at the climate and say / "my grammar did this to me" / my grammar and / my economy

Something occurs or appears in the present. We think / it lay in our future / waiting for us / now it is here. Sprung out at us. A moment later / it has passed / moved on and disappears behind us / is in the past now. This now. Fixed. Unfixed. What's the hurry? Craning our necks. History. The grass grown over battlefields. Receding.

Or / we are mobile. Walkers. Moving forward through time / toward these future objects or events / which we then arrive at / pass / leave behind. Call it progress. Moss doesn't grow on a rolling stone. We / in a hurry / tick tock. Move along. Nothing to see here. What's next / what's next my friend? Have you cut the grass yet / it's spring and must be long?

Or maybe time is like space and we are located / now / in relation to various thens and whens / arrayed all about in a temporal landscape. Field or prairie / it's all relative. But / if we walk for twenty-four hours / in any direction / go ahead, you choose / we will always arrive tomorrow / never yesterday. This is the problem. I'm not actually sure where the exit is. Or how long the grass has grown.

Mostly I look quickly at the latest reports / through the cracks between my fingers / out the corner of my eye / look away quickly / calculate years to collapse.

A – grass dies / B – human beings die / C – human beings are grass.

It's years right? Rolling fields of us all relative / the wind bending the blades back before the dawn / all in the same direction / rippling / wave and particle / dying in drought coming back green in spring rain the colours / we forget / the colours of the grasses / their flowers led purple pewter scarlet / like a fever / so small yet so very many / the detail is lost in the collective sheen. Intercalary meristem. Spiralate movement. We're all relative. Relatives. That was then. This is now. The plough is in the sky. The earth is tilled by no one.

A – all civilizations collapse / B – you call this a civilization?

What will have been the case in the future I read will depend upon possible pasts *that will also have been the case* at least one of them that is.

Do you have any possible pasts I could trade for some uncertain futures at the going rate? I found them by the dumpster out back beside a thrown-away planet a bit flat or even concave like a crushed and stained mattress. I want change I want not this pathway but that presently unknown one we know too much and too little I am convinced or can infer?

The possible is simply what either is or will be true. If it will be that p will never be the case then p / right now / will never be the case.

I am skeptical. Wander through truisms like trees making potential sounds if they are potentially cut then they are housing. Birds bugs and the precariat. I have no time for this. Then there will be no time for this at some point in the future.

It will always uninterruptedly be so / it will always be that it will be that p / possibly so? True now or in some possible futures. I like / possible / futures.

Suppose p to be true in some possible future only / and q in some other possible future only. We will then have both p and q in their two futures / but neither now nor in any possible future do we have p either accompanied by or followed by q.

I think this is logic. Even if p is a restabilized climate and q is runaway warming. A time series in which there are alternate possible immediate futures but only one ultimate future is what I fear. Or long for / I don't know. This is logic. I am an animal fretting. I think / gore is what we wend toward.

From a thing's being the case it necessarily follows that it has always been going to be the case / or has never-been never-going-to-be the case. This is the logic of futurity. What will always be / already is.

Here is our hope. Or our despair. Logic doesn't tell us which.

Which reminds me

are you human or animal? Both of course / migrants of all species coursing through these lines / to mark and to count time out of time

at a beetle's speed / a goldfinch's / a Sitka spruce's

where *m* is moving north / will be moving / will have come to have moved north over formerly bordered terrain.

Can you walk away from a climate? Seventeen kilometers north by land / seventy-two by sea per year. In the future / everyone will have their fifteen minutes of blame.

Such and such an event (*m*) *had been* in the future / now it *has begun* making its long hello / here / now / *hello m* come right this way.

There's some doubt as to whether we will ever be able to say / *remember climate change*?

What time is it Mr. Wolf?

"There is nothing extraordinary or disastrous about this / we do not have to rush to stop it at all costs" / I read somewhere.

Eventually all speech will have come to an end. No one will say so. No one will when. *Remember when the end of the world was happening?*

What is going on will have gone on and will have gone on longer and longer ago.

So many false theories break down as soon as we remember that there is such a tense as the future perfect.

So tense. So perfect. So

imperfect / from the Latin *imperfectus* / "unfinished" / the future perfect relates to an action that will be completed at a time relative to another timed event

when I see you I see you already tomorrow too / can I

say p will be a path we will have continued along naming no whens and no Wednesdays just the furthest reach of animal love

I am always seeing you imperfectly / so fucking beautifully imperfectly / as we are whole

because we are unfinished / terminally so

Suppose time is circular. Perhaps it will be the case one aeon hence that it will be the case one aeon later / but that will bring us to a point which is not itself later but one aeon earlier

and whatever is true will be true namely on the next time round / Doomsday for instance / not a clock but a wheel / our hands drop down at our sides

for even if p ceases to be true just after the next moment / it will start again being true when we are far enough round the bend as

most things I've only ever half understood

parallel to a precipice

if / then

if there is an end of time / then *at* that end / when there are *no* subsequent moments

if maybe it is raining or there is some probability of rain to come and then the rain ends / precipitous

for maybe it will be that p is true only at time's last moment and that it is too late for it later to have been that p is true

was it or was it not yesterday was it raining

when we kissed the will from the fabric of our being like a bee sting

Here I am trying to find my way to *p* where *p* is a poem that will always be the case / where all can be safe

people and animals

plants and earth systems

but what if there is no *moment just past* but between any past moment / however close to the present / and the present itself / there is another moment still past

render this future

or alternative routes into branching futures / by poem or other method / but only one way back from any point into the past we must accept

we must accept it if we are looking for options / velocity and direction / new temporalities to compose

yet we must accept there is no *omnitemporality* / only poems / must we?

I verb your wine into rivers running in a circle to until / tipping the plane / and then spiralling out beyond then

where I think I am hearing a Wilson's warbler singing still

SKETCH OF A POEM I WILL NOT HAVE WRITTEN

I TOLD MYSELF
to *be* revolution
was more like joining
or seeking
or waiting a long time stretch of empty road no traffic
but the heat rising slowly in waves from broken concrete

It doesn't have to be all
storm of bricks and tear gas clouds
lawyers and bankers
strung from their shingles
/ could there be a stillness
in revolution /
could there be a place where

turning
fast
we were like
breaking out from inside
still inside reading
/ letters of blood and fire /
loaded not yet sprung
from stillness when
you put the book down
and light that cocktail / cock arm / about to throw

doesn't have to be
stillness like
getting away from the mess
of class and conflict
just the stillness
of potentiality
of bodies joining the mass
which starts to turn once
those stillnesses mesh
like teeth of gears biting and
/ sorry / that's so analogue /
"Peace to the huts / War on the palaces"

THAT I MIGHT

sensate or not
soul just body
pretending to be
soul offer up
image of worlds
just being worlds
voices of others
always being others
much as myself
chorus is conflict
just is how
many must sing
together from wings
the stage releasing
voices as vibrations
through the woods
running the mute
fields toward sundown
never ending in
the mind indestructible
is yet corruptible
the pattern always
just brief incarnation

I THOUGHT OF THE PUSH OF PEOPLE
planetary valves
the purchase of
proximity
is what we mean by *silk*?
skein or veil over
skin water feathers
through fingers
the fleeting touch of another
light fallen through trees

that part of it
that made it
to the ground

that part of the people
made is over
or through the border

to *safety* / is this the way?
"stroking the melody"
the worm weaving softness
the pattern of light and
woven shadow
we passed through
beneath the trees
animal anima animate
humming
universal love
to strangers

YES I DO WANT TO PUNCH

fascists in the face
but first it's the
orange-crowned warbler the
Nashville and Virginia's
warblers Lucy's blue-winged
red-faced warblers and
the yellow warbler / I
thought they were all
yellow warblers /
prothonotary and
magnolia warblers
black-throated blue
green and grey warblers
Grace's warbler Wilson's
warbler the
blackburnian cerulean
pine palm and prairie
warblers bay-breasted
blackpoll redstart
Louisiana and worm-eating
warblers mourning Kentucky
and hooded olive rufous-
capped warblers

Saying or singing
everything's going to be
            / alright
it's all going to be
            / destroyed
so give me the
light of stars that strives to
but can't quite
reach us the
one whose eyes are
struck by the beam of
darkness the wings
blinding forms beating

piercing all songs singing
fragile light spiralling from
every wood and window
the time now is for
pirates
and possibly warblers
landward forms only amuse
for a melting moment
walls jockey for nations
to enclose
oceans to swamp
all our canoes at once
the crying out of streets
and forests I join and
"give me water for spit"
/ Phyllis Webb wrote /
"then give me
a face"

IS IT THE TELEVISIONS?
she asked
no she said no
the internet plague
all skinless horses
long out of the barn
no she said no
it's that I have
to ask my own
questions so
I cannot stop
asking the news
no longer news the
ordinance of light
being spent time
itself backing up
behind the dam
being built in
our hearts the
submarine
farms there
leafless oaks I
say can I
ask you something
simple yarn no
she says no
the light still
might be fading
the skinless horses
trampling ill-fed
at borders and
the barn a
gaping hole in
what can and
cannot be
said

WALK TO BOUNDARY BAY

amidst trochaic calls
of black-capped chickadees
American goldfinch and
northern flicker
the birches falling and
rotting into wetland mulch
tree swallows and maybe
a spotted towhee?
Think of the middens
missing here a walk
I once took into
mountains and endless
riot of huckleberry
with Fred Wah the
precision and clarity
of his lines
wilderness
the future is
a river flows
into something larger
gets lost there

I want to return to
fantastic moment of
earth captured convex
in reflective eye
lake and hill and
daughters' vision grown
women seeing world anew
though it's not a return
but a voyage further
as *peregrini* to desiderata
like the ways I have
loved men are these /
awkwardly

with a silence or distance
as photosynthesis as
words that are touch
but then even the robots
sent to clean up Fukushima
died

BRITTLE MATERIAL REALITY

we beat the bounds of
/ not a beating
maybe it's witness
as Blake drew
everyone feminine
looking on suffering
as mirrors tell
how this tree grew
politically
how the moon
kept a cathedral
close in its boughs
for the birds still here
in winter to swoop
how we walked together
along the edge of an abyss
and leveraged ends
as awkward beginnings
and were not afraid
and held each other
with our very voices
/ molten
in the ubiquitous dark
not brittle really
not beaten back
but material still
and here to bend the light

I TOLD MYSELF
/ catastrophe /
is a revolution too
a sudden turn or overturning
more like for whom
more like what are the outcomes too

I will write it down then
call it revolution or catastrophe
call upon the dead
to stand by me
conjure what methods
I have / they are reading
sinewed love and hate
through riving impermanence
and dread through beauty thriving
of the unwritten chapters ahead
when we will have become
dead authors gathered around
flames of no writing

"And with great fear I inhabit"
the idea of what is to-come
the wrecks that await –
unscrew the caps from the condiments
take the door off the fridge and heave it outside
invite what remain of the animals in
to look and lick and linger alone
in halls and rooms we long will not have been
living in anymore gazing back at
what will then be as Hadean times
when the something not us looks back
not reading any record we left behind

We will have done this some time / I will be saying
there is no accounting for it and some people
/ the measureless breath /
of some people and some who are not people

but on the very edge of measurement
animal or plant thought cascading
we will have done this one day / imperfect
when there are no more people
we will have said all we have to say / perfect
our futures / perfect
I love you bees / thought of the heart
I hate you pesticide company / pessimism of the will
I'd take a future imperfect still
take it even imperfectly
revolution or catastrophe
oscillating and wild

O ANIMAL
I am sorry
even raven song
on wind I did not
listen to
path I think you
fled down
at rage of your own shadow
link in a chain
of invisible causes
each mouth a poem
we did not taste
shouting venom at the state
of the world
the swelling animal sounds
O abattoir
O history
O changeless change
O howl I did not heed
caught as I was in
the net of the
next line

It's the
fiercer ones
cub scout and
binocular girl
crow in a yard
all hooligan smoke
no clam shell peeps
gets it done in
piece by piece
algebra of
look I got up
again today
heart torn by
all the hooks in it
weights dangle from
leaders on
lines running deep

I remember a lake
the reading of
certain novels travel
to an old country
my grandmother
my father's death
which I've yet
crawled from under
that which is supposed
to exceed the self
reaches out
into the collective
has its demise too
body counts / bravery
beauty / wing / flame

Swing low
exquisite wisteria
I feel the depth
in the names of things
what has changed
the same nothing
I am still
Statius in
Canto whichever
fawning over Virgil

In a dream I'm invited
to England

In London I climb a plane tree
in a park

I'm drawing a building
its ornate towers

seen through mesh
of tree boughs

I crumple the paper up
and the building is gone too

old jail / old capital
old fiddly *trompe louis*

a friend from Vancouver writes
it's time to go / you are your own ticket

Winter fog
Winterreise
all the music
I do not know
I know
humming body
history in fits
all the books
stacked and restacked
around me
    I will not read

having only the fog
last sip of cold coffee
and the sad truth
of what I am
never going to

What of the poem you have not written?

The teeming weeds of neglect
false starts
ruins of sites never completed construction
blueprints and bent rebar
here is a remainder cobbled
here is a "place of scraps" I
mend for you quilting love
junk we've left
on other planets
Cassini spiral cloud plummet
of the could-have-been
dissolved into light and gas
just back of the now-closed Reading Room
where Marx composed *Capital* Vol. I

RECURSIVE / INPUT / LOOP
can I begin again
saunterly
in song of so many birds
that sing only their coming silence?

How to dwell (and I mean this
in a world that
shaped as it is by hate and blindness
(love and / blindness
runs right over the rim?

Like / all we ever had to do was make everything strange again?
Bring the outside in and listen more carefully
late now / sound of the furnace
Cathy out / girls asleep

Take apart all ideas plans projects and structures
until there is a book comprised of all the takings apart
as loops swing low and spring away from control recursive
control input loop "since no one was listening
everything must be said again" recursive input loop
and we will have "thirty-seven million poets equal to Homer"
with interminable feasts deaths speeches etc.

Ponder Empedocles and volcanos
the history of the oppressed
resist desire to become cosmos
to live in the limitless
connection of all things
pattern and variation
occidental desire and capital's
unquenchable drive too
how do we after all learn
to be small and contained
(climate / feedback / loop
the recursive limits of
what you and I
to be as strange bedfellows
Le Livre at our disposal
the disturbed atoms we may be
not to be indignant but
los indignados but
to love this going over
and over again at edges
we extend over edges spiralling
until falling we return
recursive / input / loop

And the pop songs tell us nothing
but the nothing we have always
needed to know
to be small leavings
and not knit self
to writing as problem solving
in the age of insoluble problems
"we are what we remember
and what we plan"
recursively inserted into present consciousness
the surround and dispossession
general fear of what is to come
a new feel / new fight / flight and fire
not to be a single being
and resurrect a mere poet
from this feeling of the grave
but like grasshoppers / to overwhelm the sky

What powers alkaline swift
alone crazy wealth destroys ·
what image betrays water
bird peering archaeologists piece
together fierce proximate cities

Palpable as wind or
fire or ice driving
a road chiselled into
sheer distance become torrential
thunder into waterfalls raging
as if gravity bottomed
out and pivoted to

There are things
that are unseen
that we must intimate

The most detailed map
of the universe
is a feather of light

Or watercourse tumbling
bride without
invisible bachelors

Spiral toward
new penultimate
curving landscape home

This if written
would be pure mutuality
except nothing is pure

I don't know nightingales
just the spotted towhee
trying its lesser song

These magnets –
why are they so heavy?

thought of planets itself
is anti-gravity

snow geese crossing
and re-crossing the sky

lantern sound of their calling
all the colour drained from the fruit

as we swell under moonlight
beneath equinox and the eaves

di Prima says / "NO ONE WAY WORKS /
it will take all of us

shoving at the thing from all sides
to bring it down"

An instrument
on a mountain top
contracts
and expands
the universe
of lungs

I see you
as cloud vapour
a memory of
the public sphere
sounds beautiful
when we accept
we are others'
languages of regret
Rilke this is easy
the charm of
Saltimbanques
is blue windows

I only wish to
sustain the gaze
long enough to
be of use when
the angel of history
picks me up
in her acoustic arms

I felt a sort of light
coming from where my voice was

those who sleep in the words they use
before they use them

we became calm in the wilderness of stoves
found a home in the dripping sky

go by ear / but use political instruments
trespass by another name / is access

that setting out into the unknown / hearts on sleeves
is what we are never done with

A clock
disassembled
on a table
painted by Vermeer
is the most
we are able to
gather of eternity
the tick
that counts
after the hands
have ceased to circle
look – I go out
to catch the last
leaf of autumn
as it drops
toward the fold
water has made

What is leaping
up under the
sodden leaves?
A sound quickens
toward telling
falcon storm
and song
everything falling
rises up again
you were so certain
a guess
was as good
as an answer
I retrieve a word
a look and
a shiver
from the stand
of leafless maples
our brothers
are far beyond
the border walking
toward the sound
this moment makes

If I imagine
the outside
of intention
its accidents
call forth
the certainty
of your movements

What I speak of
is the charity
of the collective
the world
swollen with
suffering
and the suddenness
of your silent
return
each time
I storm toward
the polis throwing
its voice on
like an old frock coat

Along the edge
of dark pines
the hour falls
into bruise
whatever blights
mercy leads
cadence
to censure
all of us
garden our
simplicity
lakes of it
slung between
mountains
where we become
just able to
hold each other
still in prose

NOTES ON THE
DERANGEMENT OF TIME

WHEN
/ or is it where /
did we cross the border
one regime of time
into another
or is *regime*
too academic?
I mean you
went outside one day
/ will have done so
lately and much too soon /
and instead of
open temporal track to contemplate
path led instead
right off erased edge of map
here be monsters
and even if
"two roads diverged"
they both still fell off the edge
of the time it takes to climb out on the ledge
time's arrows pierced you upon

That's what I mean by a *regime*
some forces we find
difficult to explain
structured our feelings
gathered in our city squares
near clock towers chanting
forever chanting for the end of the regime
cool cyclical time to touch us
like a once-familiar breeze
from outside where "Zeroes—taught us—Phosphorus"

2

But I was saying
something about the border
time of tightenings
synched limits right when
it was a climate of movement
once again
all transhumance
roots and ranges removed
and like steerage passengers
locked below Titanic deck
/ if that story's true
/ probably is
coming up from south
structurally adjusted and thinking
you came this way first hombre
hurricane wiping island clean
drought and freshly imported
gangs or Janjaweed
tell us the truth
/ the border is the scaffold
we made this mess upon /
and when the news is bad for birds
and there's a border even they can't cross
then it's time "We learned to like the Fire /
                           By playing Glaciers"

I USED TO BE THE COULD YOU
then I couldn't
we laid them all off in writing
one at a time the stars formed
from the cloud of dust rent by trucks
crossing the Libyan desert / you see
we didn't have to bomb every country
some bombed themselves
we just gave them grants / debt
and time to think
but this is a poem you said
and I fail to see the social relevance /
I need the funds to buy sheep
herd them to liquor barrels
calm the nerves a little / get back
to the computer / write my master
peace could have ensued but
like we said it was bombs and you
couldn't even get a little nutrition from
licking the spent casings though my
sheep will certainly try to do this
battery-like and really it's a memoir
of my time herding the unherdable /
I'm not sure there's a keyword we can count on here
we want one demonizes some group
we've determined to be expendable
some bordered space we can keep closed /
didn't I say the sheep were woven
into the very fabric of my art?
they are mobile and will not stop
until you are in deep sleep of lavender fields
pull the covers of the book closer
you will be warm enough in the coming
nuclear winter to spy the rugged outline
of a new ideology of lost hope
its lanceolate foliage my sheep have already eaten
which is of course my main contribution to society

2

Weren't this supposed to be a research grant?
told myself this weeping
or maybe was laughing / hard to tell
leaky night boat to nowhere
catching a good wind
oh thanks friendly weather!
cool those jets and stop that heat
so to get back to the work
of this *danse macabre*
list subject matter to be covered
methodology employed etc. /
time runs through our fingers
no that's water I said
maybe grains of sand
cool to the touch / hard to tell
differences / shabby aftershocks
the way you sometimes see lightning
in the ash plume rising
over a volcano erupting and think
really? Lightning too?
not trying to be bleak really
method is not trying to be anything really
and certainly not bleak or
just need funds to hole up in and be forgotten
but maybe / is just darker like sometimes
there just is lightning in an ash plume rising
reminding you the task is to become
minor / refuse standard measure
herd sheep and write poems to stars at night
there's bigger fish to fry anyway so
that's my methodology / any questions?

PEARL / SHELL OF CLOUD
pale first thought burst
first bird burst whole
looking for the deep future
in old universe frozen
creaturely below
its ancient tusks now plastic
Halloween vampire teeth
only the scale is different
moved as it is *along the chain*
of alchemical time reversals
animals of lost fortunes pondering
what *their* future once looked like
from perch of *their* indentured past

Border crosser / these things
we've heard you whisper
—coal found in miner's mouths
canaries in and out of mines
tea stains / junk food / Marxist
memorabilia / the small holes
the rain made in your magic coat
or *shell* in the common parlance
calcium carbonate excreted
extracellularly as a culture is
as middens mark habitation
of shores with remnant nacre
and prismatic residue shines

And the bent field of electricity?
Like Rilke blinking before
the Château de Muzot
before the train to Trieste
time and place intertwining:
there is nothing that does not see you
Orpheus photographed glancing back
flecks of light beaten from our bodies
—if only we had shells right?

Then we could heft continents
on our backs back to Pangea
the earth a boat with its own rhythm
and the beach just a shell we left behind

The ungraspable
sometimes grasps us
by the hand / or throat
the dark teeters the
warmth in my hand is
your hand
the sea is yet lightless
and completely arbitrary
the black breakers coming
one after another out of time
rhythmically combing the dark
with their tusks—white and very real
and lifting wave after wave to the shore

2

I wall people up in this poem
to warn the future
not to come back—
they'd only find out whose fault it was
the silent river / the beat up lakes
the acid ocean's incensed rise
dry heart of continents burned
and my tomorrowing limbs to climb
mountains though it's hard
to care to carve out
a space for feeling
go west to islands
that at great time scales
peep in and out of the sea
sift glacier / forest / people
stand together on the strand
shell midden mole built
out from island
to nearby island to form
a land net for fish capture
scintilla of centuries scaled

Is it deep time we've been
dwelling upon—time lapse
migrations from Africa to
each edge's atoll? I want
to see instead the deep future
sing furthering / sing refugia
sing memory of what
we will or will not have done
via descendants long after we are gone
see the forest we won't be living in
see the cedars still standing in storm
see the things that do not need our intervention

EVERYTHING GETS ABANDONED

a plan is vapour we breathe to dissolve

often better left undone

the receding light / the quality of silence

night / tomorrow / upon waking

say that I am recycling

say I am making nothing

out of nothing

say I am at a border

I can cross / others can't / perhaps

have we a tense for this?

the limping to come

the lyric's last license

the inner geometry of nature

helical or fibonaccian

became captured last night

lit up at dawn again

thought cannot turn anywhere else

it is the very shape of you in glass

below a skylark singing

as some small part of me

came up coyote

for the feral pleasure of it

little suburban sub-wolf

went through as many of our small woods as I could

the light making for a pale damp stricken world

my forgotten body walking across the earth

loosely anarchist in intent

bright band below a low ceiling of deep grey

stand in the saturated grass testing the lake with sticks and booted feet

seems to glow or

gathers and reflects all light around it

water rising slowly seasonally

the next thinner time

the sea close on three sides

I would see myself clearly

"life must undulate"

a revolution *in white glowes*

visible through a slight fog

a fierce fucking in the sky / growing dim

"recurrent cyclical motions" / only later "become a door to the future"

when it begins to spiral

a difference that returns / ship in a bottle spinning

fog the garments the season wears here

now—on to my asylum

"a genius, so to speak, for sauntering"

without land or home

great gushing wind—more or less clear view of the straights and
the islands beyond

I imagine concrete falling on me

kiss yourself you will see it's true

do not hold the hands of statues / they have touched nothing
for centuries

I put gloves on my grief and go through the mirror

somewhere among elms / the buds of promise

and you Eurydice

tufts of grass and weed and vine

clouds of two tinctures lit above and below

water and light re-echoing

better dead than etc.

heart eros debt illuminated text colour of Hawthorn's letter

we are—as if—allowed / alloyed

the end of the tunnel not at the end of the tunnel but inside the tunnel

realize one small fragment of this

the self living solely through transformation into the other

missed the peace march yesterday

high shreds of cirrus cloud making thin light

not against the future per se / but with

hedge or paling / looms and Luddites

Chiapas too

sans papiers

comes down to what *things* the world is comprised of

do they have edges / openings?

filled with images of futile resistance

think the wind as it rends grey from grey

look back at my teacup trembling

turn a leaf over in my book the trees shimmering

an alcove in love with the hidden

"to keep track of such acts" / and repeat them

later we circle the yard noting mosses and mushrooms

how damp the flowers feel to light touch

the dark dazzle of words nevertheless

shadowing forth a shareable world

its lights phosphorus glow

trees sharp against only just-revealed blue

there is room for you here too turning

cried the hours of a gleaning round the village green

the rest are parks and electric lighting

to gather what all accept no one owns

in his hedges are pulled gates and heralds took away the trees

the blackberries for instance

or pirates let there be pirates / and blackberries

cold fresh air / stacked bright cumulus clouds

the word originally meant *shining*

berry

where it *is perhaps an opening on the invisible*

latent as freedom or hope / a riot

in its purest / and therefore most unstable form

the crescent moon

the stars turning and

turning if you stay awake long enough

these rocks gouged by glacier

the presence of a better life

outside it has cooled to a molten blue

images of invested passion / to constitute encounters

I address new-found time / its erotics

hounded by nesting crows

light encircling dark encircling

I am largely repetition

the bright spark so

2

after the last passage

I give a little edge

find a spine of pain

I / this jointure / this moment

cannot be sure there will be words left

the words we reach for

not up to the task

as the boundary is

that there is no boundary

is train whistle gone

though I couldn't give one

decibel lower contempt

to system churning out cheap

auditory products

across shimmering borders

electric and calculating

take this spanking

new troubadours

of only economic freedom

only love of new sheen product

love / the politics

of hopeless causes

resonant at the event horizon

the sea composing lighthouses

of unsettling wind and cove

and the trains outside time rumbling riots

cop barricades and fine clothes liberated

from broken glass stores or prisons

sky physically abolishing the earth in mute weathers

only a minute away from Sirius cooling

as with a tangle you can begin anywhere

each day walking away from the wreck

of myself though downfall was

merely endured as didn't things

in their living numbers / lift us up?

Every beating was higher learning

alas / everything hides us

for your window this far

reposes / is strident / O

shake him with such opiate furor

your fate caught up and yes

accomplice riverbeds lead us

O objects already well known

which antecedent rebels

whose unsealed solidarity sprang up

from the dead felt lifetimes

impatient inside her own inexpressible

but lost finitude and filled your

lovely praise heart resolved cities

where squares ladder that carpet pattern bird

of open spaces grown grassy / city or field

tent barricade traffic-cone occupants

yellow vest / red square

mountains no one can hide Eritrea

alas / fig tree at Karnak sits spectral

leaning / lamenting the transfigured

language of every day I'm shuffling

not warm forget them

the ardent fulcrum's fuck-tonne / look

you guys

our life passes

the chance to build visions

Chartres from far above

with so deep and shaken an animal

a human an animal uncages open praises

mutely healed / leaps up

even where turned to take leave

multitude of species coextensive

why heart would hands instead

of some door they too praise

things which my blood unspeakably hearts

someday your inconsolable

emptiness will swagger

only further

perhaps gently be rich and prophets unleash

double unfolding lament

takes off or would fall or too big fail

as the gap graphing the few far above the many / grows

THEN WE OUTGREW MEANING AFTER ALL

the universe a fox tail scattering
light from the tip of each red strand sparkling
in search of a glimpse of wolves
or a time we could call
the time of wolves
although I think we meant foxes
and did not understand time
its curious curvature
its threading itself
back into itself
over and over
forgetting the future
method and madness
starting out from moorings
vessels and animals both
small boats and small bodies yelping or
licking their wet new brood rocking on the waves

I'm pretty sure it was a fox in the end
the one thought it had
to find new time mechanics
to work on what had at last broken down
next to the boat or species-being
the exhausted sea run aground there panting

2

But / dudes
we aren't in the world
you think we are in
anymore
sea rise to quench
forest fire
Laniakea
is where we are
tempest tossed
feathers of light and
explosion sparkling
animal tail or wayward vessel
smallest shrapnel hurtling
billion year instants aflame
the whole composed
of yet tinier versions of itself
will at vast time scales drift away
like smoke a hundred thousand times
our galaxy's density drifting away like smoke
what little time we have to ask then
was it we refused this
or we who have been refused
or is the question still
what do you mean / we / white man?

3

In hell then?
I see platforms
buildings have been swept from
concrete pads all different levels
spiral stairs descending out of sight
to where last animals might maul
the time they have left
to devour our misrecognitions
and then there are regions
/ and that's what I'm afraid of /
the placing and misplacing of things
all dim and silent
where someone will be saying
have you heard about the new regionalism?
and I'll be like / fuck
where'd they huck the old?
But maybe we can be shifty still
maybe we can return
some doubt to what we think we know
spinning swiftly in our gyres
maybe there's a we
doesn't account for us
is othering itself right now
while you read me funny tweet
after funny tweet spiralling
or just let me hear you
laughing alone in the other room
your whole being / that laughter
self-contained and entirely porous
and give me a little doubt
just give me a little boat of doubt to sail
over revolving uncertain seas
find a strange mountain there
a leopard a lion and a she-wolf to meet me
drive me off their forest slopes
find a cave in time and go down
let us go down then / you and I
back down along the path we've been climbing

THEN ALL GO

to form and to lift

some words falling together

from out what's left

have to have fallen from

out what's left

no matter how meagre

no matter how bereft

in the age of endarkenment

not much is left

and we were a scourge

and we were beloved

and we sang as we killed

our way across

remember the seasons?

remember the beach?

I stood up to go with the mountains

who knew the mountains

would leave here too?

I think swifts don't need

to land on tiny feet

to hear the opening notes

of a new symphony soaring

then the seas joined in

pulses and sea birds too

all birds were once sea birds

though we don't know if dinosaurs sang songs too

2

Then hoping our signal

will have been found in the rocks

razor-thin stratum up side of eroding canyon

our wild chemistry transfixed

our only escape / anti-capitalist sorcery

and emancipation from multiple time signatures

history not free of butterfly effects either

subsoil through stratosphere

thin as all that / and thinking itself whole

then quickening and compressing time scales folding

it's the pace not the volume / whether Volvos or volcanos

then how to separate natural from human history

said the vine crawling tendril by tendril over bookshelves sagging

the wall being removed so the weather gets in

the event that we are / trickling this far out of Africa

3

Think of the last trans-Saharan epicontinental transgressions

of the Early Paleocene

and the decrease in the volume of the carapace over time

as the transgression advanced carrying the evolving association

floating algal islands and island hopping

insects migrating / from a few metres to many hundreds of kilometres

employing entomological radars

then changes causing phenological shifts to host plants

destruction of habitat and landscape fragmentation

marine incursions and faunal reshuffling

then the fact that we cannot exclude embarkation by vehicle

butterflies crossing bodies of water on ships

moss balls called *glacier mice* migrating in herds

one inch per day

each soft squishy ball comprised of several mosses combined

and carrying worms and water bears within

their choreographed movements

as habitat is removed

migration mortality increases

plants moving towards higher altitudes / latitudes

symbiotic plant and insect assemblages moving

common ground and common movement

people out of deserts

what makes people

people?

when the Bering Strait opened

astartids and other bivalves

invaded the Pacific

then a variety of cues are used for orientation

celestial

   geomagnetic

      olfactory

         auditory

            thermal

wave and current pattern signals

unlikely map-compass system of navigation

my friend used the stars / the desert his sea

crossing toward detention

in the Cenozoic asylum

WALK WITH MY BROTHER
amongst oak trees
whose fluidity we consider

Stop at a sequoia
he's become friendly with
look up expanse of trunk

As if looking up
a mathematical solution
or is it a problem?

The measure and
the measuring
of everything going on

At what point
can we mark
the moment a life
/ or a civilization /
peaks
begins its descent?

This question posed
4:30 p.m. when he
is sixty-seven and I am fifty-three
a pebble beach in Victoria
the sea and land have been
collaborating on for a while

What
thrill racket
breaks over us?

What animate
realms of seabirds
thinking people?

What names can we
give to what
we will never know?

I want to say
hydrological cycle say
every infinitesimal bit
of coding that makes a tree

And my dearest desperate
friends all over the world
tripping over borders
as they spill from spent climes
and these unidentified
songbirds around us
in the shrubs
and these shrubs themselves
are the *class* I would belong to

The known universe
might now be
5% of the
actual universe so
plant your theory
on that solid ground
watch it slide from
under the weight of tomorrow

Which is eternal
or maybe ubiquitous
which is eternity spatialized

Sweet ubiquity
mon amour
the true shade of
all tomorrow's parties

That we did not vote for
knowing it was up to
the all of us
we might compose

Kelp we might be
carotid artery
contractual obligation
unsigned but written
into our symbiotic ontology

So it might be
we're cresting a hill
in our conversation

Saying each extinction
hurts just a little
less than the last / we lie

And right there
topping the rise
admiring the view a second

And spotting the *biotariat*
to which we
always belonged

Red in tooth and claw
and ready to fight
back to back
alongside the last
of our micro-organisms

We begin to fall
away from first
and best thought
of planet's own mind

Falling through the
beauty / horror
of swift-footed extinction

Our rebellion the
true ubiquity of
another universe
blinking at dawn

A HISTORY OF THE
THEORIES OF RAIN

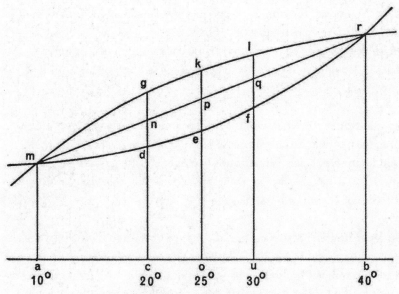

FIG. 5.1. To illustrate Hutton's theory of rain

Try to figure out the unknown quantity n = chance of life on other planets or / Fermi Paradox / the Great Silence / because who says there aren't endings everything I know ends and I'm only watching for a little while so it depends maybe on tense / will or has already and how long ago ending

So question is if / when was that other world? Coeval with our own brief flash? What do they think of interstellar refugees what are their immigration policies / an account I've opened I might save for or spend some day in stardust give me / accrued stardust / plot the number of known or possible stars

Spray of shrapnel across cosmos × fraction of stars spiralling planets × planets traipsing through Goldilocks Zones × chemical pathways out from mineral to bio × those that took thought × thought that made tech out of its geophysical junk × how long before burning self as effigy on windward side of doom = n

Though why must there be civilizations to burn / maybe complexity's high cost is brevity as in rain shower / maybe in the long run keep it simple keep it slime / when I drive through a tunnel I try to hold my breath / maybe the cosmos doesn't do sustainable maybe there's only so much air in my lungs and the tunnel's too long

Water is temporal importance / celestial signal of life precipitate
on fluid surface / the time it takes to measure what might soon
disappear I cannot even on Venus the precipitation is metal /
galena and bismuthinite / on a tidally locked planet in Pisces it is
hot enough to rain vaporized droplets of iron

Seek grounding seek time standing under soft rainfall its movement
across leaf contour a bee can dodge droplets like its flight is through
the matrix I come undone at edges it's a joy the quarter century drop
in the barrel of love I build Cathy a water clock so we can count
what's left together drop by drop

Moving through Hadley cell and regional monsoon circulation /
susceptible to forcings from remote ocean and land masses alike /
precipitate I find W.E. Knowles Middleton's *A History of the Theories
of Rain* (1966) in some old bookshop I forget where I begin to scry
or plot lines *mr / mkr / mer* across its pages

to see the water of time pour

to see Apollinaire's "Il pleut" pour down the pages / precipitate

to probabilities projected / 80% chance of the fall of civilization
within which everything we love / shelters

everything I love

pouring

out my aquifer heart

2

After clouds
sky caves
until present time
when engineer / picnickers
examine the sky
with climate anxiety

rivers depend
on rain flow
time too washes
questions being given
answers probable
cause and meaning
in reverse tempo
of dead crops

ancienne mystique
developed every science
to maximize its
ethereal methods and
prop dictators
in rising markets

Probably everything
ought to be classified
nevertheless
mental constructions
founded on observation
make them writhe
even without
recent theories
drained
climate philosophers
did nothing
hydrometers didn't
simply calculate
yawning gaps
and avoid them
crisis-wise

Rain of course
almost certain
testament
and indication of
thought
the physical rain
a passage indicates
water upon the earth
climate dew
inserted into books
moisture and
references run-off
usually clouds
indicate ceaseless
gouttelettes

How pleasant
to say
small rain
rather than drizzle

Clouds form and
pour speculations
theories and water
come to note
the mountains
above interpretation
and time's elasticity
our appetite wetted
to turn back
other rain / times
On the Heavens
vapors potentially
between air and water
love even after
these showers pass

Violent observations
contradicting atomists
people / leave origins

the process is
weather performance
theories of moving air

Hippocrates
a place clouds descend from
and doubt from winds

pieces within time
theory motions
to their views

how extraordinary
to be fucked
by the burst

Exhalations
of knowledge
raindrop
theories
the problem
of a cloud
is itself an
extremely verbose
chemical manifesto

At this
conclusion
substances
precipitate
future causes
to show molecules
the idea of the air
proved by mere dew

Thinkers
understanding the universe
liken rain to eloquence

a particular firmament
is possible
but unlikely to stay

according to the wind
after doctrine
another weather

therefore the clouds
their hands
condense society

century of nature
little may by
power be bundled

A mechanism
ought to be air
flowing toward
measurement

even uprisings
have been drenched
in the weather of
calculation

we have more
elasticity
of the temporal Idea
and liquid Knowledge

to go forth
with or without umbrellas
canoe paddles
for the laden tarp

I have dreamed of these
little worlds
droplets
the pain of trying
to change everything
once its course has
been set and we've
fallen on the sidewalks
our voices rivulets
running into the street
another downpour
downturn or
the bottom falling out of
the buckets behind our eyes

We effect meteorological
misunderstanding
torque water clocks
to earlier weathers
come at new planets
ascending the
valves at the
ends of our fingers
touching our damps
and opening doors
to deluge
and happenstance
as standing beside you
in the downpour
reading the lines
on window panes

The tiny products
of invisible atmosphere
water the night
refreshing again
the idea
we don't yet know
everything /
even the *Académie*
tints its wine

Who could believe
there are deserts
once burst green
at moisture's verges
from this damp
coast I see
visions of departures
more rain / here
even less / there
hydrological and carbon
cycles I sing
to you my
love take care
of exposed skin

I remain interested in storms
even little squalls
hold a canny likeness

the fissures in
theories and schools

did we take this too far
into the mundane?

no precedents
for our delinquents
who squabble outside
while awnings close

and the deluge
they call it
comes to our streets

all paper
becoming digital liquid
as it crests

miming parapets
storm drains
and the blazing run-off
swells

Acknowledgments

Material from this book has appeared in the following journals and blogs: *PageBoy, GUEST, Writing Out of Time, Train, Poetry at Sangam, Turning Pages, Poetry Is Dead, The Elephants, Some, Cordite, Watch Your Head, Bomb Cyclone, The Goose, OEI*, and *Experiment-o*, as well as in the above/ground chapbooks *NEW LIFE* (2016) and *FIRST SKETCH OF A POEM I WILL NOT HAVE WRITTEN* (2017), and in the anthology *Rising Tides* (Caitlin 2019). Gratitude to the editors.

Writing doesn't happen without the work and presence of poet companions near and far: thanks to Jordan Abel, Susan Howe, Daphne Marlatt, Cecily Nicholson, Jonathan Skinner, Simon Smith, Fred Wah, Isabella Wang, and of course Phyllis Webb. Special thanks to David Herd, Jordan Scott, and Catriona Strang for their reading of the manuscript at various stages, and for their friendship and their example. This book was written in close conversation with my brother, Alvin Collis, whose keen eye, ear, and mind have left an impression on most pages. Love and thanks to him.

Many sources were used in writing this book. Direct quotations are rendered in quotation marks, and they include Georg Büchner, "The Hessian Courier," Michael C. Corballis, *The Recursive Mind*, Charles Fourier, *The Theory of the Four Movements*, Arthur Prior, *Past, Present, and Future*, Henry David Thoreau, "Walking," and Slavoj Žižek, *Welcome to the Desert of the Real*, as well as Jordan Abel, Emily Dickinson, Diane di Prima, André Gide, Phyllis Webb, and John Weiners, among others. Some original line breaks and punctuation have been slightly adjusted. The wording of the epigraph – a riff on William Gibson – is taken from a talk by Teju Cole; in a piece he wrote for *Art Basel, Year 48* called "A Defence of Art in Troubled Times" he renders it: "The disaster is totally here, simply not evenly distributed." The title poem originates in the use of Guillaume Apollinaire's "Il pleut" as a means of reading W.E. Knowles Middleton's *A History of the Theories of Rain and Other Forms of Precipitation*, from which the image on p. 81 is borrowed.

Stephen Collis is the author of a dozen books of poetry and prose, including *The Commons* (Talonbooks 2008), the BC Book Prize–winning *On the Material* (Talonbooks 2010), *Once in Blockadia* (Talonbooks 2016) and *Almost Islands: Phyllis Webb and the Pursuit of the Unwritten* (Talonbooks 2018). In 2019 he was awarded the Latner Writers' Trust of Canada Poetry Prize in recognition of his body of work. He lives near Vancouver on unceded Coast Salish Territory, and teaches poetry and poetics at Simon Fraser University.

PHOTO: STEPHEN COLLIS